D-DAY TO VE DAY

MONTH BY MONTH

Published by IWM, Lambeth Road, London SE1 6HZ
iwm.org.uk

ISBN 978-1-9124-2391-0

A catalogue record for this book is available from the British Library.

Printed and bound by Gomer

Colour reproduction by DL Imaging

EU Authorised Representative: EAS Europe - Mustamäe tee 50, 10621 Tallinn, Estonia, **gpsr.requests@easproject.com**

Front cover: IWM (B 10172)/artistic rendition 2025

Back cover: IWM (A 23938)

WORLD LAND TRUST™
www.carbonbalancedprint.com
CBP2275

MIX
Paper from responsible sources
FSC® C114687

D-DAY TO VE DAY

MONTH BY MONTH

June 1944 – May 1945

PETER JOHNSTON

IWM IMPERIAL WAR MUSEUMS

CONTENTS

INTRODUCTION

On 6 June 1944, for the first time since 1940, the Allies returned to north-west Europe in numbers and force. The long-expected invasion of France, which had been planned in earnest since 1943, was finally underway.

Operation 'Overlord', the invasion of Normandy that had been planned and unleashed with such detail, ingenuity and secrecy, was the largest amphibious invasion in the history of warfare. In preparation for D-Day, British factories substantially increased the production of supplies and equipment, Canadian forces had been built up in Britain since 1939 and over 1.4 million American servicemen arrived between 1943 and 1944 to take part in the landings. Over 2 million troops from over 12 countries were in Britain in preparation for the invasion by 1944. This strength was being built to deliver the first of several hammer blows necessary to defeat Germany.

Shortly after midnight on 6 June, over 18,000 Allied paratroopers were dropped into the invasion area to provide tactical support for infantry divisions on the beaches. The Allies used nearly 7,000 naval vessels, including battleships, destroyers, minesweepers, escorts and assault craft, to land and support more than 150,000 troops on five beaches. Allied air forces flew over 14,000 sorties in support of the landings and, having secured air supremacy prior to the invasion, many of these flights were unchallenged by the Luftwaffe.

Establishing a bridgehead was critical, but it was just the first step. In the three months after D-Day, the Allies launched a series of additional offensives to try and advance further inland. These operations varied in success and the Allies faced strong and determined German resistance. Even the eventual success in Normandy – itself no simple thing – did not end the war in Europe. It was only the beginning in the drive to victory, the start of a long and arduous campaign to liberate north-west Europe from the tyranny of Nazi occupation. The Allies had to drive Nazi forces from France, Belgium, Luxembourg and the Netherlands, and then fight their way into Germany itself. It would take a further 11 months before Germany surrendered and peace was officially declared in Europe, ending the most destructive war in the continent's history. This hard-won result was greeted with celebration in Britain and across the Commonwealth. It brought an end to six years of war in Europe that had had caused significant trauma trauma and suffering to so many people.

In Britain, the day – Victory in Europe Day – was declared a public holiday. In towns and cities across the nation people marked the victory with street parties, dancing and singing. Similar scenes occurred all over the British Empire and Commonwealth. But as they celebrated, people also mourned their lost friends and loved ones.

Of course, there wasn't only fighting in north-west Europe during this period. D-Day in Normandy wasn't even the first D-Day of the war; troops in Italy had faced their own D-Days at Sicily, Salerno and Anzio, and were engaged in a dangerous and difficult advance up the Italian peninsula. Operations in Italy had their own challenges, and combat was just as fierce as in France, Belgium, the Netherlands and Germany. In the skies above, Allied air forces continued the strategic bombing of German industry, fuel, transport and housing infrastructure. This had begun piecemeal in 1940 but was expanded into systematic area bombing raids by hundreds of aircraft at a time. Designed to break Germany's ability and will to resist, the raids devastated around half of the built-up areas of its major cities and towns. In Eastern Europe, the Soviet Union was waging its own war on Germany at a massive scale on the Eastern Front. The Soviet Byelorussian offensive, Operation 'Bagration', was launched just after 'Overlord' and destroyed the entire German Army Group Centre. These campaigns together served to weaken German resources everywhere, leading to their eventual defeat and a truly Allied victory.

Further afield, British Empire and Commonwealth forces were engaged in South East Asia. Between December 1941 and August 1945, British Commonwealth troops and their allies fought a bitter war against the Japanese. The fighting took place in malaria-ridden jungles during drenching monsoon rains and on remote islands in searing tropical heat, but always against a tenacious and often brutal enemy. On 7 June, the day after D-Day in Normandy, British and Indian forces began the drive from Kohima in north-east India to lift the siege of Imphal – the defining moment of the Burma campaign and the point at which the advance to victory began there.

The focus for this book, however, is about June 1944 and the weeks and months that followed in north-west Europe, and predominately the role played by those personnel under British command. The western Allies had made the defeat of Germany their principal war aim as early as December 1941, and it was only through the north-western European campaign that that goal could be realised. This book uses the incredible photographs in the archives of IWM to follow the forces of 21st Army Group, and the Second Tactical Air Force and the Royal Navy, across France, Belgium, the Netherlands and Germany itself. 21st Army Group, under the command of Field Marshal Bernard Montgomery, was a united nation: it included soldiers from Britain and Northern Ireland, Canada, Poland, the Netherlands, Belgium, Luxembourg, France and Norway. 200,000 of them would become casualties in the campaign.

This force fought its way across fields and forests, rivers and fortified towns in an advance from the beaches of Normandy in France to the shores of the Baltic in northern Germany. This book covers the triumphs and the tragedies of that time, the brilliant successes and the terrible failures. It shows ordinary people living through extraordinary times, in the crux of the greatest war ever fought. And it shows them delivering victory.

JUNE

On 6 June 1944, the Allies launched the largest naval, air and land operation in the history of warfare. Codenamed Operation 'Overlord', but better known as D-Day, it marked the beginning of a long and costly campaign to liberate Europe from Nazi domination.

The defeat of Germany was acknowledged as the western Allies' principal war aim as early as December 1941. The British Empire and Dominion forces, and the Americans, had been fighting an attritional campaign against the Germans in Italy since 1943 – a campaign Churchill had optimistically referred to as 'the soft underbelly of Europe.' But it was not going to deliver the knockout blow the Allies wanted, or weaken the German efforts in the East as Stalin had been demanding.

Opening a 'Second Front' in north-west Europe was seen as the key to victory. It would relieve pressure on the Soviet Union in the East, and the liberation of France would weaken Germany's overall position in western Europe. The invasion, if successful, would drain German resources and block access to key military sites. Securing a bridgehead in Normandy would allow the Allies to establish a viable presence in northern Europe for the first time since the evacuation from Dunkirk in 1940.

Detailed preparations for Operation 'Overlord' began in late 1943. A command team, led by the American General Dwight D Eisenhower, was formed in December 1943 to plan the naval air and land operation. As a crucial part of their preparations for D-Day, the Allies developed deception and misdirection campaigns to draw German attention and military strength away from Normandy. This included fake radio traffic and decoy equipment, such as inflatable tanks and dummy landing craft, and even imaginary military forces and special agents.

To build up resources for the invasion British factories increased production, and in the first half of 1944 some 9 million tonnes of supplies and equipment crossed the Atlantic from North America to Britain. A substantial Canadian force had been assembling in Britain since December 1939, and over 1.4 million American servicemen had arrived between 1943 and 1944 to take part in the landings. By 1944 over 2 million troops from 12 countries were in Britain preparing for the invasion. On D-Day Allied forces consisted primarily of American, British and Canadian troops but also included Australians, Belgians, Czechs, Dutch, French, Greeks, New Zealanders, Norwegians, Rhodesians and Poles.

Early on the 6 June, Allied airborne forces dropped behind the beaches to secure the flanks of the landing zones, then at 6.30 hours troops began landing on the five assault beaches: Utah, Omaha, Gold, Juno and Sword. The eastern invasion force was made up of British troops, landing at Gold and Sword Beaches, and the Canadians, landing at Juno. These beaches were closer to Caen, which the Allies were planning to liberate. The British met with relatively weak defences and succeeded in meeting up with the paratroopers dropped earlier, holding their positions and fighting off German counterattacks. This was not the case for the Canadians at Juno. The heavily fortified defences and rough seas meant that they suffered more than a thousand casualties.

By the end of D-Day, over 160,000 Allied troops and 6,000 vehicles had crossed the Channel. Getting them across the Channel and ashore had been the first obstacle. Now, the second major obstacle needed to be overcome: keeping the war machine supplied. Until they could capture a major port, the Allies had to rely on two artificial floating harbours to supply the invasion force. These were built in sections and towed across the Channel for final assembly at the main beachheads. Mulberry A, at Omaha Beach, supplied the Americans until it was destroyed in a storm on 19 June, which further delayed the Allied breakout from the beachheads. Mulberry B, on Gold Beach at Arromanches, was used by the British and Canadians. It remained in service for 10 months, allowing 2.5 million men, 500,000 vehicles and 4 million tonnes of supplies to be unloaded.

D-Day was a success for the Allies, but many of the immediate strategic objectives of the landings had not been achieved. While the Allies were backed by enormous air and naval firepower, and had more men and resources than the Germans, the enemy still controlled most of Normandy. 'Overlord' was about more than just getting ashore. There would be weeks of hard fighting ahead as the Allies attempted to turn the landings into a successful advance.

JUNE 1944

Sun	Mon	Tue	Wed	Thu	Fri	Sat
..	..	..	..	1	2	3
4	5	6 D-Day for Operation 'Overlord'	7	8	9	10
11	12	13 The first V1 flying bomb hits London	14	15	16	17
18	19 Storm hits the Mulberry Harbours	20	21	22	23	24
25	26 Operation 'Epsom' begins	27	28	29	30 Operation 'Epsom' ends	..

MONDAY

05

Four 'stick' commanders of 22nd Independent Parachute Company, British 6th Airborne Division, synchronising their watches in front of an Armstrong Whitworth Albemarle of No. 38 Group, Royal Air Force (RAF), at around 11pm on 5 June.

TUESDAY

06

Troops of 3rd Infantry Division on the Queen Red sector of Sword Beach at around 8.45am, 6 June.

TUESDAY

06

Above Troops from 50th Division coming ashore from LSI(L)s, Gold Beach, 6 June.

Opposite An aerial photograph of Horsa gliders near the Bénouville Bridge over the Caen Canal that, along with Ranville Bridge over the River Orne, was seized by troops from D Company of the 2nd Battalion of the Oxford and Buckinghamshire Light Infantry in the early hours of 6 June. The soldiers had been delivered within yards of their objective by Horsa gliders flown by the pilots of the Glider Pilot Regiment, achieving total surprise and success. The bridges were later renamed Pegasus and Horsa.

4007
16/412:6JUN44:20"//K18.

TUESDAY

06

HMS *Ramillies* carrying out a very heavy bombardment in support of the eastern flank of the Normandy beachhead during the early stages of the Allied landings. Her powerful guns were employed during the assault in neutralising coastal batteries and later broke up dangerous attacks by German tanks and infantry.

TUESDAY

06

Troops of 9th Canadian Infantry Brigade disembarking with bicycles from LCI(L)s (Landing Craft Infantry Large) onto Nan White beach, Juno area, at Bernières-sur-Mer, shortly before midday, 6 June.

TUESDAY

06

Canadian troops of B Company, North Shore (New Brunswick) Regiment, take cover behind steel girders and logs guarding the approach to the German strongpoint WN-27 in Saint-Aubin-sur-Mer, 6 June.

WEDNESDAY

07

Reverend Victor Leach, Padre of 13th/18th Royal Hussars, leading a burial service for a fallen tank soldier killed in action with the German 21st Panzer Division near Hermanville-sur-Mer, 7 June.

WEDNESDAY

07

A Cromwell Mk V tank of 4th County of London Yeomanry, 22nd Armoured Brigade, 7th Armoured Division, leads a column of armour, including a Sherman Firefly and soft-skin vehicles, inland from the King sector of Gold Beach, 7 June.

TUESDAY

13

Rescue teams and civilians help to recover a casualty after a V1 attack at Clapham in South London on 13 June, the day the first flying bombs hit London. Facing a deteriorating strategic situation in Normandy and on the Eastern Front, Germany deployed its 'revenge weapons' (*Vergeltungswaffen*) in a bid to terrorise British civilians and undermine morale.

HR

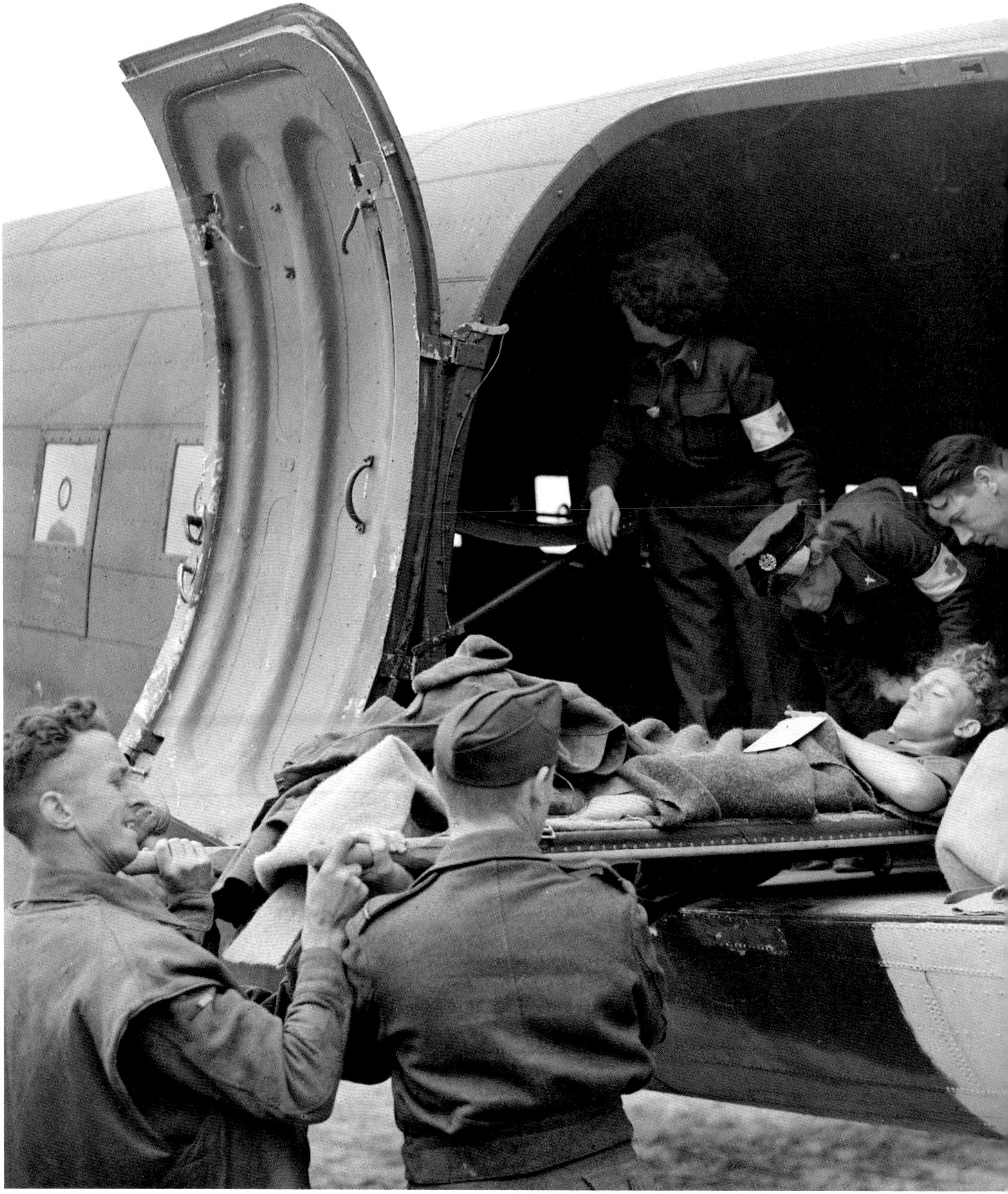

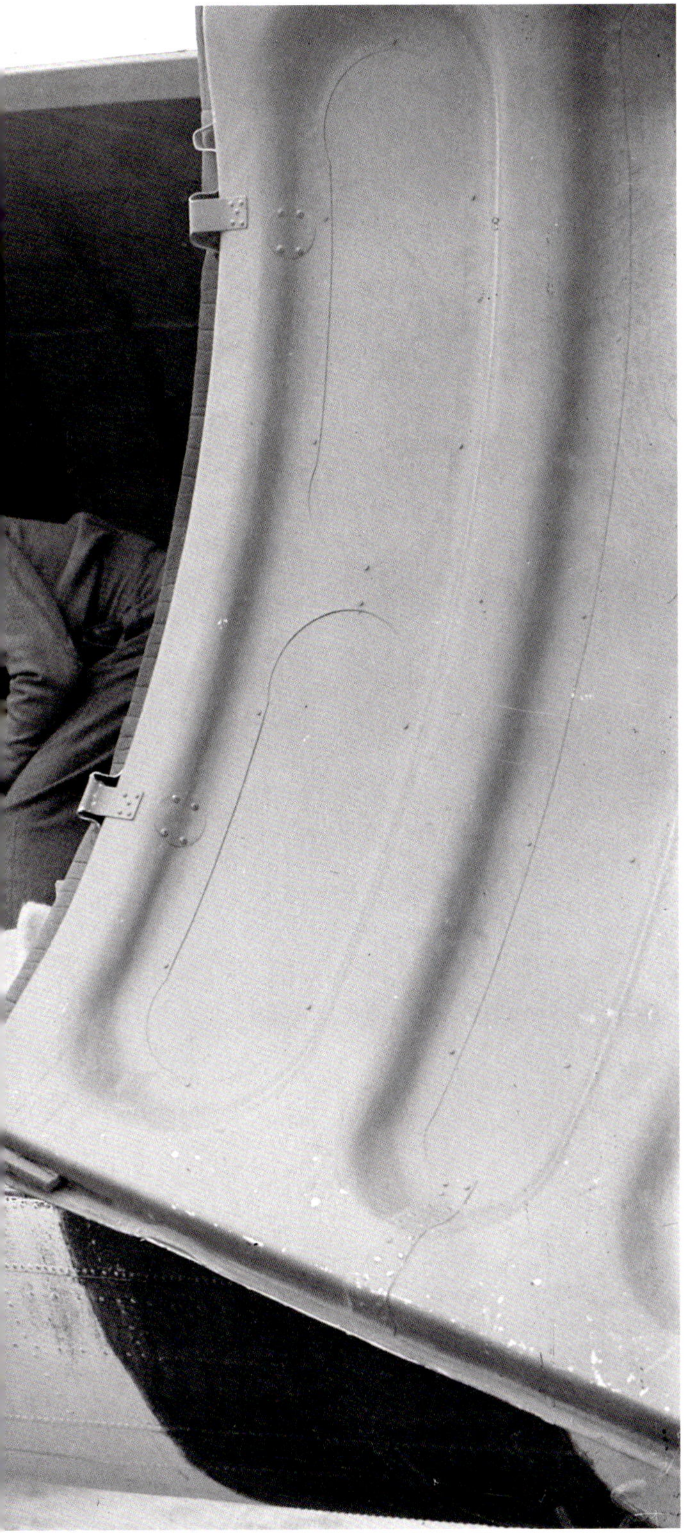

TUESDAY

13

Aircrew and Women's Auxiliary Air Force (WAAF) nursing orderlies help to load a battle casualty on a stretcher into a Douglas Dakota Mk III of No. 233 Squadron RAF at Bazenville (B2), Normandy. The RAF's first 'casevac' flights to France were mounted by Dakotas of No. 46 Group on 13 June, and the WAAF nursing orderlies pictured were the first women to be employed on these duties.

WEDNESDAY

14

General Charles de Gaulle, the leader of the Free France government-in-exile that had been established in the UK in June 1940 after the French surrender, addresses a crowd in liberated Bayeux immediately after arriving in France on 14 June.

MONDAY

19

On 19 June a fierce, three-day storm hit the Normandy coast. The Mulberry harbours were exposed to its full force and the American's Mulberry A suffered so severely that its breakwaters were largely broken up and work on the harbour was discontinued. This image shows damage to the floating causeway of the British Mulberry B at Arromanches-les-Bains as a result of the storm.

MONDAY

26

Troops from the 6th Royal Scots Fusiliers in the village of Saint-Manvieu-Norrey during Operation 'Epsom', 26 June. Epsom was launched to outflank and seize Caen from the Germans. The strain of battle is apparent on the soldiers' faces. The infantry faced the hardest of tasks, vulnerable to machine guns, mortar fire and snipers. These soldiers are carrying pickaxes on their backs to help dig the slit trenches that were their only protection.

MONDAY

26

Men of the 7th Seaforth Highlanders, 15th (Scottish) Infantry Division, on the move during Operation 'Epsom', 26 June.

WEDNESDAY

28

THURSDAY

29

Above
A Churchill tank of 7th Royal Tank Regiment, 31st Tank Brigade, supporting infantry of 8th Royal Scots during Operation 'Epsom', 28 June.

Opposite
Infantry of 8th Rifle Brigade (Motor), 11th Armoured Division, move forward cautiously near Éterville, Normandy, 29 June.

JULY 1944

In July, the major focus for the Anglo-Canadian forces was to capture Caen, so that they could seize bridges over the Rivers Orne and Odon, and launch the breakout of the beachhead and the advance inland. Caen had been an objective on D-Day itself, but the British and Canadians had failed to capture it. Fighting the previous month around the city had failed to dislodge the German defenders. Caen needed to be taken, and the Germans driven out and tied down on the Allies' eastern flank.

In Normandy, Montgomery was determined to fight a battle that minimised the weaknesses of his own forces and instead made use of Allied advantages in firepower. He knew that the supply of replacement personnel would be limited, and keeping casualties to a minimum would be a priority. His motto was, 'Let metal do it rather than flesh.' Above all, Montgomery sought to instil confidence and maintain the morale of his men, which he believed to be the most important single factor in war.

As the capture of Caen was fundamental to the Allied plan in Normandy, plans to seize the city were revised, and an enormous bombardment was launched from land, sea and air on 8 July. More than 650 artillery guns opened fire and over 2,000 tonnes of bombs were dropped in a raid by 450 aircraft of RAF Bomber Command. Typhoons provided tactical air support, and naval gunfire support was provided by four Royal Navy ships in the Channel, including HMS *Belfast*.

This bombardment reduced much of Caen's historic city centre to rubble. The impact of this bombardment, and its necessity, has continued to be debated, but the effect on the residents was devastating; 80 per cent of the city was destroyed, and 3,000 civilians were killed. The Anglo-Canadians succeeded in occupying the northern part of the city, but the Germans fell back to strong defensive positions on the high ground south of the city.

Following Caen's capture, Anglo-Canadian forces engaged in a series of exhausting battles to the west of the city. These included the fierce fighting over the high ground known as Hill 112. Combat was intense, casualties were high, but neither side had a clear advantage. On 18 and 19 July, the British launched Operation 'Goodwood', this time to the east of the city, as the Canadians simultaneously launched Operation 'Atlantic'. These were major actions involving thousands of soldiers, guns and armoured vehicles, as the British and Canadians attempted to hold the Germans in battle, wear down their forces, and allow their material advantage to tell. The Germans committed most of their forces to battle against the British and Canadians rather than the Americans in the west.

Yet it wasn't without cost. 'Goodwood' saw the British and Canadians suffer 5,500 casualties and lose almost 500 tanks – about 36 per cent of the British tanks in France. 'Goodwood' may not have been the breakout Montgomery desperately wanted, but it kept the bulk of the German forces in the British sector. When US forces launched Operation 'Cobra' on 25 July, they subsequently faced weaker German forces. 'Cobra' broke open the German lines southwards from Saint-Lô, and American forces began their advance westwards into Brittany and eastwards towards the Seine.

To support this advance, Montgomery launched Operation 'Bluecoat' on 30 July. Sensing a turning point, his orders to his commanders were to, 'throw caution overboard... accept any casualties, and to step on the gas.' 'Bluecoat' saw savage, costly fighting, but the British were learning and improving their operational skills, and finally had the advantage.

JULY 1944

Sun	Mon	Tue	Wed	Thu	Fri	Sat
..	..	..	..	..	..	1
2	3	4	5	6	7	8 Operation 'Charnwood' begins
9 Caen is captured	10 Operation 'Charnwood' ends	11	12	13	14	15
16	17	18 Operation 'Goodwood'	19	20	21	22
23	24	25 US forces launch Operation 'Cobra'	26	27	28	29
30 Operation 'Bluecoat' begins	31	..	..	..	..	..

SUNDAY
09

A group of some of the first British soldiers to enter Caen on 9 July pose with some of the French civilians who had stayed in their homes, despite the fighting that destroyed so much of the city.

SUNDAY
09

A British soldier on the lookout for German snipers hiding in the ruins of Caen as the city was being cleared, 9 July.

SUNDAY

16

A Royal Artillery 5.5-inch medium gun firing at night during the offensive in the Odon Valley near Évrecy, 16 July. Medium artillery regiments (each containing 16 guns) were corps level assets and were normally used to supplement the infantry divisions' own field regiments of 25-pounders. Their heavier shells were more effective against dug-in enemy positions and were crucial in Normandy for generating and maintaining momentum for any advance.

SUNDAY

16

Infantry occupy slit trenches in the forward area between Hill 112 and Hill 113 in the Odon Valley, 16 July.

TUESDAY

18

Opposite On 18 July, 927 RAF heavy bombers took part in raids to attack German positions ahead of Montgomery's Operation 'Goodwood'. Here, the Handley Page Halifax B Mk III, LW127 'AL-F', of No. 429 Squadron Royal Canadian Air Force, flown by Flight Lieutenant George W Gardiner, is seen in flight over Mondeville, France, shortly before it crashed. The aircraft lost its entire starboard tailplane to bombs dropped by another Halifax above it. Three of the crew were killed, one evaded capture and three became prisoners, including Gardiner.

Above A 56-ton German Tiger tank from the 503rd Heavy Tank Battalion blown upside down during the Allied bomber attacks that preceded Operation 'Goodwood', 18 July. Despite the devastation caused by the bombing, most of the battalion's Tigers escaped serious damage and by the end of the day had knocked out 40 British tanks.

WEDNESDAY

19

Soldiers of 1st Welsh Guards in action near Cagny, during Operation 'Goodwood', 19 July.

THURSDAY

20

Aircrew of No. 166 Squadron gather round Wing Commander D A Gardner at RAF Kirmington, Lincolnshire, on 20 July to hear a congratulatory message from Montgomery, thanking the bomber crews for their efforts supporting Operation 'Goodwood'.

MONDAY

31

A column of Sherman tanks of 2nd Irish Guards, Guards Armoured Division, move across country during the advance south of Caumont, 31 July.

AUGUST 1944

The objective of Operation 'Bluecoat' was Mont Pinçon, the highest point in Normandy. Despite heavy fighting, British forces advanced rapidly, and by 6 August the summit of Mont Pinçon had been captured. 'Bluecoat' and American advances further west left the German forces in Normandy weakened but still capable of fierce resistance. A final German counterattack was launched in an attempt to halt the US advance on 7 August. But without adequate air support, it had little chance of success and failed, broken up by overwhelming Allied firepower. A general retreat of German forces began.

A pair of Canadian-led attacks, Operations 'Totalise' and 'Tractable', including British and Polish units, rapidly followed. The Canadians advanced towards the town of Falaise with the aim of meeting up with General Patton's US forces, advancing from the south and cutting off the German retreat. Falaise was captured on 16 August after heavy fighting, and the retreating Germans soon found themselves trapped in a shrinking pocket, coming under devastating aerial and artillery bombardment. However, the Allies were unable to fully encircle and trap them. Many of the German soldiers managed to escape before the pocket was finally closed on 21 August after bitter fighting, though 60,000 were killed or captured and nearly all their guns, tanks and vehicles were abandoned.

On 19 August, the French Resistance began an uprising in Paris as the US forces approached, and the Germans from Normandy retreated through the city. Eisenhower had wanted to concentrate on the destruction of the German forces and bypass the city entirely. However, Charles de Gaulle, the leader of the Free French forces – made up of those French soldiers and civilians who had escaped from France, Belgium, Norway, and North Africa from June 1940 – convinced Eisenhower to detach the French 2nd Armoured Division from US command to liberate the city. By the morning of 25 August, Paris was free. De Gaulle paraded through the city the following day to scenes of jubilation from a population that had endured four years of occupation.

Further operations continued in the British and Canadian sectors, and the first British troops crossed the Seine on 26 August as part of the headlong advance by Allied armies across eastern France and Belgium in pursuit of the collapsing Germans. On 1 September, Eisenhower took direct command of all Allied ground forces: the Battle of Normandy was over.

Normandy was one of the most intense and bloody campaigns ever fought by the British Army, with casualty rates at times rivalling those of the Battle of Passchendaele in 1917. Between D-Day and the end of August some 83,000 British, Canadian and Polish troops became casualties, with almost 16,000 killed. All seven of the British and Canadian infantry divisions that fought in Normandy had lost three-quarters of their initial strength by the end of August. The rifle companies had been the hardest hit. Though they formed no more than 20 per cent of the army, they had taken 70 per cent of the casualties. In an echo of the First World War, junior infantry officers had a mere 1 in 10 chance of surviving unscathed. At times the British struggled to replace the casualties and were facing a manpower crisis.

But by the end of August 1944, the Allies were virtually at the borders of the Reich. Surely Germany couldn't continue to fight much longer in the west?

AUGUST 1944

Sun	Mon	Tue	Wed	Thu	Fri	Sat
..	..	1	2	3	4	5
6	7 Operation 'Bluecoat' ends	8 Operations 'Totalise' and 'Tractable' begin	9	10	11	12
13	14	15 Operations 'Totalise' and 'Tractable' end	16 Falaise is captured	17	18	19
20	21 The Falaise Pocket is closed	22	23	24	25 Liberation of Paris	26 First British troops cross the Seine
27	28	29	30 Operation 'Overlord' ends	31	..	..

IN 60
H.O.
64

WEDNESDAY

02

A Sherman tank of one of the British armoured units passing through ruins of Cahagnes, during the advance towards Aunay-sur-Odon, 2 August.

WEDNESDAY

09

Men of the Durham Light Infantry move up during the fighting south of Mont Pinçon, the highest point in the Calvados region of Normandy on 9 August. It had been captured on 6 August during Operation 'Bluecoat,' which led to a collapse of the German positions in Normandy.

SATURDAY

12

The fighting for Mont Pinçon was hard. While the British eventually dislodged the German defenders, they suffered many casualties. A cemetery for those killed was built by German prisoners of war (POWs) at the foot of the high ground, in the village of Roucamps. In this image British soldiers are making crosses to mark the graves of the fallen on 12 August, after the end of Operation 'Bluecoat.'

TUESDAY

15

A Cromwell tank of 2nd Northamptonshire Yeomanry, 11th Armoured Division, driving through Vassy, France, 15 August. 11th Armoured was making good progress at this time, advancing south as part of VIII Corps on the British right flank. At the end of the month 2nd Northamptonshire Yeomanry was disbanded and most of its tanks and crews posted to 7th Armoured Division. Its place in 11th Armoured Division was taken over by 15th/19th King's Royal Hussars.

TUESDAY
15

A military policeman with two attached Auxiliary Territorial Service (ATS) 'Redcaps' – Corporal Joyce Collings and Lance Corporal Cecilia Strong – watch over traffic near Bayeux, 15 August.

SATURDAY

19

German vehicles, caught in the open and attacked by the Allied 2nd Tactical Air Force, burn on a road in the Falaise area, 19 August.

SUNDAY
20

MONDAY
21

Opposite
A German StuG III assault gun on its side in the river after falling from the bridge in the village of Putanges, France, 20 August.

Above
A Sherman tank crew, smoking a variety of pipes, awaits the order to advance near Argentan, France, 21 August.

MONDAY

21

Two soldiers of the 3rd Infantry Brigade (1st Polish Armoured Division) examine the masses of German vehicles and lorries piled up on both sides of the road after the Battle of the Falaise Pocket ended on 21 August.

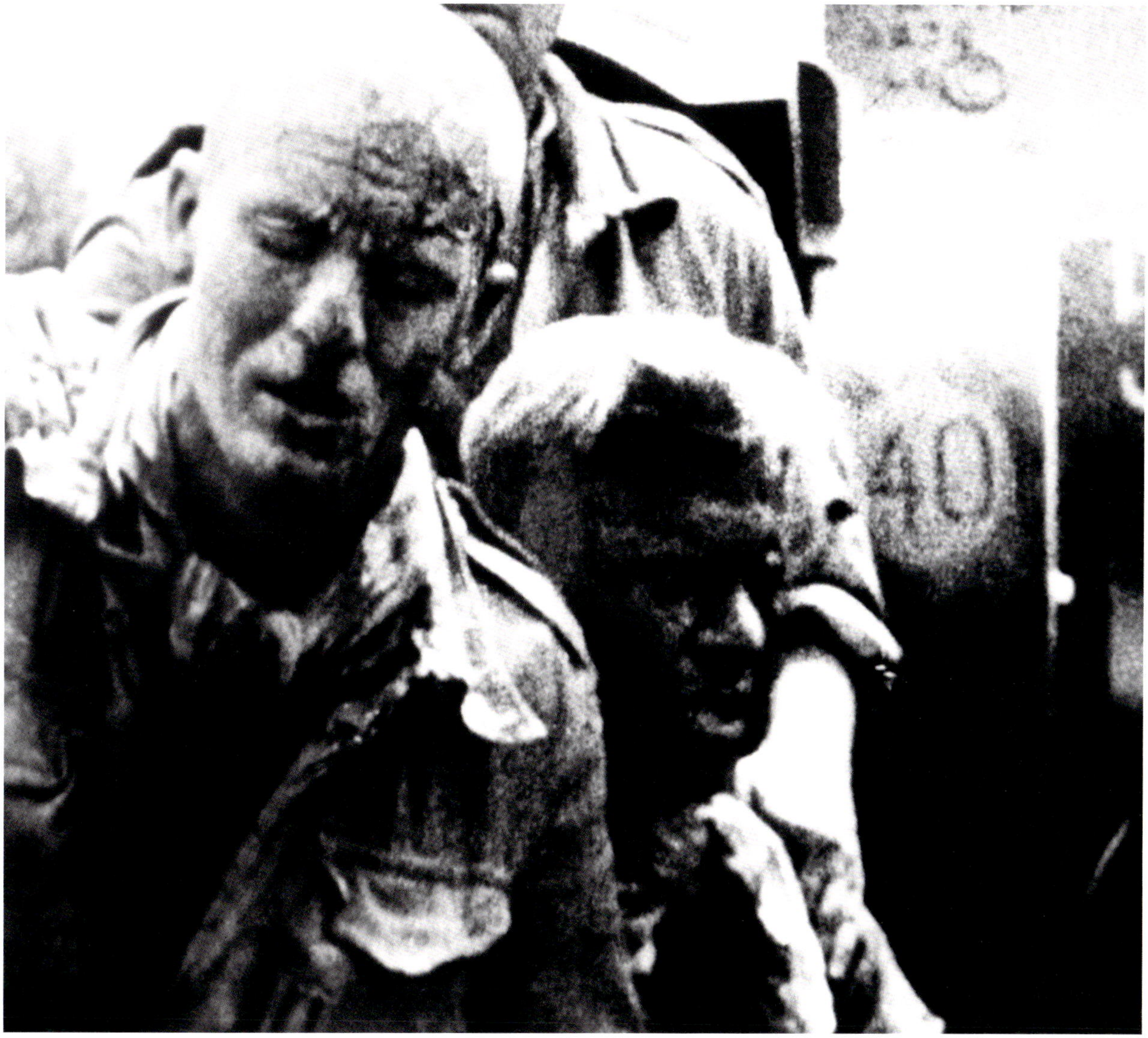

MONDAY

21

Troops of the 2nd Armoured Regiment (10th Armoured Cavalry Brigade, 1st Polish Armoured Division), showing their exhaustion after the Battle of the Falaise Pocket, 21 August 1944.

TUESDAY

22

A French civilian who had remained in Lisieux during the fighting pours a drink of cider for a Bren gunner in action, 22 August.

FRIDAY
25

While de Gaulle was in Paris, British and Canadian troops were in contact in Normandy. Here, British troops approach the banks of the Seine at Vernon ready to cross by boat, 25 August.

SATURDAY

26

The day after Paris' liberation, de Gaulle led a parade from the Arc de Triomphe down the Champs-Élysées to Notre-Dame cathedral for a service of thanksgiving.

SATURDAY

26

French civilians run for cover as German snipers open fire as de Gaulle reached Notre-Dame cathedral during his parade through Paris on 26 August.

SEPTEMBER 1944

Allied divisions had advanced after the fleeing Germans so quickly through Normandy that they eventually outran their own supplies, and in early September the pursuit was brought to a halt so that formations could be replenished and refuelled. The Allied armies stood at the borders of the German Reich, with the British and Canadians in the north and the Americans to the south. Allied commanders now argued over the best strategy to finish the war, and who was to be in the vanguard.

Eisenhower wanted to continue the advance on Germany along a broad front, but logistical issues meant the Allies couldn't simultaneously supply multiple Army Groups with the fuel, food and ammunition they needed. While Antwerp had been captured on 4 September, it was not usable until the Scheldt estuary was cleared to the north.

Montgomery, commanding Allied ground forces, tried to persuade Eisenhower to concentrate the available resources for a direct, narrow thrust through the Netherlands and into northern Germany, bypassing the main enemy defences of the Siegfried Line. Three Allied airborne divisions would drop into the Netherlands and secure territory and bridges in and around the towns of Eindhoven, Nijmegen and Arnhem. This would create a corridor along which British XXX Corps would advance, supported by other formations on either flank. After reaching the furthest bridge, over the Lower Rhine at Arnhem, the way into Germany's industrial heartland of the Ruhr would be clear. Montgomery argued that his plan, Operation 'Market Garden', would put the Allies across the Rhine on Germany's frontier in a few days and possibly end the war by Christmas 1944. Eisenhower was convinced, and the operation was launched on 17 September.

The airborne troops seized their objectives, but a combination of poor communications, poor intelligence, delays, bad decisions and unexpectedly strong German resistance slowed the advance of the ground troops. The British troops at Arnhem of the 1st Airborne Division, the far tip of the advance, were supposed to holdout for four days. In the end they held for nine, but they couldn't be reached by XXX Corps. Despite efforts to reinforce them, including the drop of the 1st Polish Parachute Brigade, they were forced to surrender after suffering huge casualties and running out of supplies in the face of overwhelming German attacks.

The battle would become one of the most controversial episodes of the Second World War, featuring daring assaults, strategic blunders and heroic defences. A battle that came so close to success, but ultimately ended in failure. The war wasn't going to be finished by Christmas of 1944 after all. The western Allies resumed Eisenhower's broad front strategy, and the Rhine wasn't crossed until March 1945.

SEPTEMBER 1944

Sun	Mon	Tue	Wed	Thu	Fri	Sat
••	••	••	••	••	**1** Eisenhower takes direct command of all ground forces in France	2
3 Liberation of Brussels	**4** Liberation of Antwerp	5	6	7	**8** The first V2 rocket strikes Britain	9
10	11	12	13	14	15	16
17 Operation 'Market Garden' begins	18	19	20	21	**22** German forces in Boulogne surrender	23
24	**25** Operation 'Market Garden' ends	26	27	28	29	**30** Germany forces in Calais surrender — The Battle of Overloon begins

FRIDAY

01

21st Army Group was advancing and fighting across some of the same battlefields as their fathers a generation before. Here, Sherman tanks of the Guards Armoured Division are passing the First World War Villers-Bretonneux Military Cemetery during their advance towards Arras, 1 September.

MONDAY

04

A British Sherman tank is swamped by jubilant Belgian civilians as Brussels is liberated, 4 September.

MONDAY

11

Two flight mechanics carry empty long-range fuel tanks to waiting North American Mustang Mk IIIs of No. 65 Squadron RAF at Grimbergen Airfield (B60) in Belgium on 11 September. Grimbergen had been liberated on 4 September and then quickly repaired and designated B60 for advanced operations by the Second Tactical Air Force. Squadrons operating from Grimbergen attacked German supply lines and later supported Operation 'Market Garden'.

SUNDAY

17

British paratroopers of the Pioneer Assault Platoon of 1st Parachute Battalion, 1st Airborne Division, on their way to Arnhem, the Netherlands, in a United States Army Air Force C-47 aircraft at the start of 'Market Garden' on 17 September.

SUNDAY

17

Aerial view from the north showing paratroopers of 1st Parachute Brigade, 1st Airborne Division, descending on Drop Zone (DZ) 'X', which is already littered with parachutes left from the previous drop, 17 September.

DRIE HOEFIJZERS BIEREN
HOTEL · RE
„DE WILDEMAN" · J. A.

MONDAY

18

Civilians dancing in the square of Eindhoven, the first major town in the Netherlands to be liberated during the ground advance as part of 'Market Garden', on 18 September. Eindhoven was bombed by the Luftwaffe the following day as Allied convoys transited through the town and the surrounding area. 227 civilians were killed.

MONDAY

18

On the morning of 18 September, the Germans launched an attack against 2nd Parachute Battalion in its positions at the north end of the bridge at Arnhem. Armoured cars and half-tracks from the reconnaissance battalion of 9th SS Panzer Division charged across the bridge but were stopped by a hail of gunfire, grenades and PIAT (Projector Infantry Anti-Tank) rounds. This aerial photograph was taken later that morning by an RAF Spitfire. A tangle of burnt-out vehicles can be seen on the northern approach ramp between houses occupied by the British troops.

MONDAY

18

A Piat gun of 'C' Troop, 1st Airlanding Reconnaissance Squadron, in position behind a tree covering a road near Wolfheze, the Netherlands, 18 September.

THURSDAY

21

A Cromwell tank of 2nd Welsh Guards crosses the bridge over the Waal River at Nijmegen, the Netherlands, 21 September. At this point during 'Market Garden', the town was in Allied hands, and XXX Corps pushed on as far as Elst, just south of Arnhem, but there it was blocked by strong German forces. Without support, the British tanks could get no further. XXX Corps artillery was able to provide much-needed fire support for 1st Airborne trapped at Oosterbeek, but little could be done to help 2nd Parachute Battalion in Arnhem.

SATURDAY

23

'Gallipoli II', a 6-pdr anti-tank gun of No. 26 Anti-Tank Platoon, 1st Border Regiment, 1st Airborne Division, still fighting hard in Oosterbeek on 23 September. The gun was at this moment engaging a German Pzk.pfw B2 (f) Flammpanzer – a flame-throwing tank – and successfully knocked it out.

SATURDAY

23

During the battle for Arnhem, the British were split between forces holding the north end of the bridge, and the rest trapped in a pocket of their own near the town of Oosterbeek. Holding on was a major challenge for both; for airborne troops operating behind enemy lines, resupply was crucial to enable them to keep fighting once their initial supplies had run out. However, the resupply intended for the 1st Airborne Division fell into German hands instead. This photograph shows soldiers using yellow parachutes to signal to Allied supply aircraft from the grounds of 1st Airborne Division's HQ at the Hartenstein Hotel in Oosterbeek on 23 September.

MONDAY

25

A German photograph showing British paratroops being marched away by their German captors after the battle ended on 25 September. Some 6,400 of the 10,000 British paratroops who landed at Arnhem were taken prisoner, and a further 1,100 were killed.

OCTOBER 1944

By the autumn of 1944, the Allies had liberated huge swathes of western Europe, and advanced into the Low Countries and the western borders of Germany. However, Germany was still in the war. 'Market Garden' had failed, and the Allies were confronted by the problem of a logistical tail that was extending back as far as Cherbourg and Normandy. It was simply taking too long to get supplies to the front to maintain the advance at scale for Eisenhower's broad front.

While Calais had finally been captured at the very end of September, the damage to the port was severe. Antwerp, the Belgian port, was the largest operational deepwater port in Europe, and represented the perfect base to plan the renewed invasion of Germany. The Belgian resistance seized the port to stop the Germans destroying it as they had with other facilities, and when the British 11th Armoured Division captured the city on 4 September 90 per cent of the port facilities were intact.

However, the port remained unusable: the canals, rivers and waterways around Antwerp towards the North Sea coast were still in German hands and defended heavily. Until the Scheldt River, connecting Antwerp to the North Sea, was cleared, along with the estuary in the South Beveland region and Walcheren Island, then there could be no build-up of resources for the attack on Germany. Delays in the investment of Antwerp with suitable numbers of troops, caused by prioritising 'Market Garden', as well as Calais and Boulogne on the Channel coast, meant the German garrison had been reinforced. The Germans had been ordered to hold the Scheldt estuary at all costs ahead of a renewed German attack on the Allies. They were well fortified with artillery positions and well supplied, due to the reinforcements made in the region following the Allies' deception plan to conceal the location of the Normandy landings.

The task of liberating the Scheldt was entrusted to the First Canadian Army, but the unique geography of the area made the challenge more daunting. Before the troops assigned from 21st Army Group even reached Walcheren Island, which had been fortified into a powerful German stronghold, they had to cross a floodplain enclosed by dikes, all below sea level, and flooded to help the defence and hinder any attack.

The plan for opening the estuary involved four main operations, starting with clearing the area north of Antwerp and ending with the capture of Walcheren Island. Approximately 135,000 Allied soldiers took part in the battle, the bulk of which were Canadians with support from British, Polish, French and American troops among others. Fighting against them were nearly 90,000 battle-hardened German soldiers, well dug-in on Walcheren Island and on both sides of the Scheldt estuary.

The first attacks on the Scheldt, spearheaded by the Canadians, suffered horrendous casualties. Having to cross multiple obstacles, in terrain pre-prepared for defence, the going was tough. After he had been rebuked by Eisenhower for not investing enough resources into the Scheldt, Montgomery increased the efforts of 21st Army Group. Progress began to be made, but it was slow.

Elsewhere, Montgomery also took over operations around Overloon, committing British forces to stabilise the line after the failure of 'Market Garden'. This was a ferocious battle, followed quickly by fighting for the town of Venray. The intensity for 21st Army Group was relentless, drawing down and exhausting soldiers and resources.

OCTOBER 1944

Sun	Mon	Tue	Wed	Thu	Fri	Sat
1	2 The Battle of the Scheldt begins	3	4	5	6	7
8	9	10	11	12	13	14
15	16	17	18 The Battle of Overloon ends	19	20	21
22	23	24	25	26	27	28
29	30	31	..	..	..	..

SUNDAY

01

Troops investigate one of the German cross-Channel gun emplacements at Cap Gris-Nez, France, after its capture by Canadian troops, 1 October. The long-range guns had periodically shelled Dover across the English Channel from 1940 to 1944. A cameraman from the Army Film and Photographic Unit can also be seen recording the scene.

SUNDAY

01

The camp for German POWs at Dieppe, France, before their onward move to Britain, 1 October.

WEDNESDAY

04

An aerial photograph of bombs exploding on the Walcheren dike on the Scheldt, during RAF Bomber Command's raid on the island on 4 October. This was part of the opening stages of a campaign to open access to Antwerp that would last more than a month.

FRIDAY

06

Father C V Murphy carries out Mass in a Dutch field on the frontline for soldiers of the British 2nd Army, 6 October.

FRIDAY

13

Montgomery explains Allied strategy to King George VI in his command caravan during the King's visit to the 21st Army Group in the Netherlands, 13 October.

SATURDAY

14

Vickers machine guns of 2nd Middlesex Regiment, 3rd Division, fire in support of the attack on Overloon, the Netherlands, 14 October. They had stockpiled a million rounds of ammunition for the attack.

TUESDAY
17

Infantry holding a position as part of the assault on Venray, the Netherlands, 17 October.

WEDNESDAY

18

A Firefly and Sherman tanks of 29th Armoured Brigade carrying infantry into position near Venray, the Netherlands, 18 October.

SUNDAY

22

Churchill bridgelayer tanks of 34th Armoured Brigade move up to the Antwerp-Turnhout canal for the attack north of Antwerp as part of operations to clear the Scheldt, 22 October.

FRIDAY

27

A Challenger tank crosses a Bailey bridge near Esch-sur-Alzette, Luxembourg, 27 October.

T 271924

NOVEMBER 1944

November 1944 began with the ongoing fighting for the Scheldt to finally open it up so the Allies could exploit Antwerp's vast port facilities. It wasn't until 8 November that the German forces finally surrendered after the last operations seized Walcheren.

It had taken five weeks of difficult fighting, at a cost of 20,873 Allied casualties, to clear the Scheldt. The Canadians, who had been the major Allied fighting force at the Battle of the Scheldt, suffered the most. The Canadian infantry, even more than the British, lacked the reserves to replace battlefield casualties. They had fought virtually continuously since Normandy, and – despite always stepping forward when asked – were suffering; some Canadian units had suffered 50 per cent casualties in October. All these men were volunteers; Canada had introduced conscription but only used conscripts for home defence, relying instead on those able and willing to volunteer to be sent overseas to fight. With domestic conflict over the issue of Canada's involvement in the war, and a society divided in its support along ethnic lines, the issue of supplying casualty replacements was political as well as strategic. Conscription for overseas service – which is what Britain had been relying on since the war began – simply could not be used as a solution. The casualties incurred fighting the European war provoked a domestic political crisis in Canada, and the lack of quality reinforcements was devastating for the physical fitness and psychological morale of those Canadians serving in the infantry, particularly in north-west Europe and Italy.

It took another two weeks after the German surrender for the Royal Navy to clear the mines left by the retreating Germans in the estuary. Finally, on 28 November – three months after the city had been liberated – the port of Antwerp was opened. When the first Allied convoy sailed into Antwerp, 7,000 dock workers volunteered for work in the harbour, and the unloading of supplies began immediately. Eventually, close to 9,000 Belgian civilians worked daily in the port unloading equipment and supplies with the Allied troops.

Antwerp was crucial in feeding 21st Army Group's war machine; some 2.5 million tonnes of supplies were unloaded there between the end of November and the end of April 1945. Without it, the advance would have been impossible. The German 15th Army had delayed the use of the port for far longer than Hitler had hoped for, justifying the German decision to hold their positions on the Scheldt. But the loss of around 10,000 soldiers as battle casualties, and a further 40,000 being captured, would prove decisive in the months to come. While the Allies were building their reserves, in Germany the situation was the reverse. Supplies, resources and manpower were all dwindling fast as German cities were hammered by Allied bombers day and night. To the Allies, it seemed that it was only a matter of time before Germany was defeated, but Hitler had ordered one final attack to try and turn the tide in the west.

NOVEMBER 1944

Sun	Mon	Tue	Wed	Thu	Fri	Sat
..	..	..	1	2	3	4
5	6	7	8 The Battle of the Scheldt ends	9	10	11
12	13	14	15	16	17	18
19	20	21	22	23	24	25
26	27	28 First convoy arrives in Antwerp	29	30	..	..

WEDNESDAY

01

DUKWs, or 'Ducks', amphibious craft making their way between the beach and a Landing Craft Tank (LCT 952) during the landing by Royal Marine Commandos on Walcheren Island at Westkapelle, the most western point of the island, on 1 November. This was the final phase of the battle to free the Belgian port of Antwerp. The remnants of a smoke screen is lingering on the beach.

WEDNESDAY

01

On 1 November British assault troops advance after their landings on the waterfront near Flushing, the Netherlands, while British warships provided gunfire support. This image shows shells bursting ahead of the troops moving inland.

WEDNESDAY

01

Dutch children watch Churchill AVREs pass through Dongen, the Netherlands, during 21st Army Group's advance on Oosterhout, 1 November.

WEDNESDAY

08

German prisoners being marched off on Walcheren once the island was secure. Some 40,000 Germans surrendered on 8 November.

FRIDAY

10

Infantry of the 1st Polish Armoured Division entering the war-damaged town of Moerdijk in Brabant, the Netherlands, c.10 November, as part of the pursuit of the collapsed German defences around Antwerp.

SATURDAY

18

A Sherman tank carrying infantry of 43rd Division advances towards Geilenkirchen their first offensive on German soil, 18 November. Geilenkirchen was an important road hub.

WEDNESDAY

22

Sherman Crab flail tanks of the Westminster Dragoons carrying infantry of 2nd Argyll and Sutherland Highlanders during the advance east of Beringe, the Netherlands, towards the German positions around their bridgehead at Venlo, 22 November.

THURSDAY
30

Oil being unloaded from the SS *Fort Cataraqui* in the port of Antwerp, 30 November. This was the first ship to dock at the port following the opening of the Scheldt Estuary.

DECEMBER 1944

Despite the success of June and the rapid advances of July and August, the failure of 'Market Garden' had ended the Allies' prospects of victory in 1944. As the year came to an end, Eisenhower was plotting how to renew the offensive in 1945 and bring the war to a close. For Montgomery's 21st Army Group, the immediate tasks for the soldiers were the stabilisation of the line through the Netherlands and the far west of Germany, and Christmas in the field. For some, this would be their first. For others, it would be the latest Christmas they spent at war away from home.

German plans for December, however, were very different. Hitler still believed that one final offensive could turn the tide. But since there was no way forward on the Eastern Front, that left attacking in the west. Hitler believed that by breaking through American lines, and then driving north to Antwerp, the alliance between the British and Americans would be broken, and they would be forced into a separate peace. The Germans could then renew the war in the east and fight on a single front.

This was a desperate view; the model for success was the Blitzkrieg of 1940 through the Ardennes that had delivered such a victory against all expectations, but the strategic situation was radically different in 1944. Germany had lost 3.2 million men since the beginning of the war and was facing critical shortages in manpower and fuel for any armoured attack. The Allies were completely dominant in the air, limiting the German freedom of manoeuvre. However, Hitler was already deluded about German capabilities, and despite the opposition of his senior generals, committed the Wehrmacht to a massive attack on the Americans.

Operation 'Watch on the Rhine' – better known as the Ardennes Offensive, or as the Battle of the Bulge, due to the press on US lines created by the attack – was launched by the Germans on 16 December. They achieved complete surprise and some initial success, making use of bad weather to negate Allied air superiority. However, the Germans were soon held up, delayed or stopped by unexpectedly strong American resistance around key transport hubs and other defensive positions.

On 19 December, Eisenhower made the controversial decision of giving the command of all troops, American and British, north of the bulge to Montgomery. British troops from 21st Army Group that had been in reserve to prepare for their own offensive in early 1945 were asked to come and support their American allies. Soldiers from the 7th Armoured Division, the Desert Rats, suddenly found themselves travelling to the snowbound Ardennes, where they took on German tanks. Paratroopers from 6th Airborne, who had fought on D-Day, were sent in as infantry, and men from the 53rd (Welsh) Division were likewise committed.

As Allied reinforcements arrived the German advance slowed down even more. A lack of fuel severely hampered their abilities to keep attacking. On 23 December the weather conditions finally started to lift, and the Allies were able to bring their air superiority to devastating effect. Counterattacks began and shifted the momentum. By the end of December, the German advance had ground to a halt.

DECEMBER 1944

Sun	Mon	Tue	Wed	Thu	Fri	Sat
..	..	..	..	..	1	2
3	4	5	6	7	8	9
10	11	12	13	14	15	16 The Battle of the Bulge begins
17	18	19	20 Montgomery takes command of all forces north of the German advance	21	22	23
24	25	26	27	28	29	30
31	..	..	..	..	..	..

SUNDAY
10

A dejected-looking Lance-Bombardier Davis and Gunner Carey, of 319th Light Anti-Aircraft Regiment, shelter from the rain and sleet somewhere in the Netherlands, 10 December.

TUESDAY

19

Gunner Jack Ward from Hertford, of 9th Medium Regiment, Royal Artillery, holds aloft two geese 'with pride and promise', near Geilenkirchen, Germany, 19 December. They're destined for the pot, to become his unit's Christmas dinner.

WEDNESDAY

20

This image of men of the 7th Armoured Division larking around behind the lines near Sittard, the Netherlands, on the Dutch-German border was captioned 'Christmas Shopping' by the photographer when it was taken on 20 December. The bullet splashed windscreen demonstrates the proximity and intensity of the fighting, despite the festive season.

WEDNESDAY

20

A little Dutch boy helps to refuel a Sherman tank near Sittard, 20 December.

MONDAY

25

Rifleman Corker, from Muswell Hill, London, of 1st Rifle Brigade, enjoys his Christmas pudding and rum in a foxhole on the frontline near Nieuwstadt in the Netherlands, 25 December.

MONDAY

25

The crew of a Bofors anti-aircraft gun watch vapour trails from British and American aircraft in the sky high above the Dutch-German border near Brunssum, the Netherlands, on Christmas Day of 1944.

TUESDAY

26

An Avro Lancaster of No. 625 Squadron RAF flies over the smoke-covered target during a daylight attack on German armour and troops concentrations at Saint Vith, Belgium, on 26 December, by 294 aircraft drawn from most of the Bomber Groups of the RAF. The improving weather meant the British could use air power to support the Americans during the Battle of the Bulge.

SUNDAY

31

A soldier from 1st Battalion, the Rifle Brigade, 7th Armoured Division, manning a .30-cal machine gun, 31 December.

JANUARY 1945

In January, the balance of momentum in the Ardennes Offensive began to shift away from the Germans. The Americans had, against all expectations, held on in their key defensive positions. On 1 January 1945, the Luftwaffe caused serious damage to Allied air bases in north-west Europe, but it sustained losses from which it could not recover. After the dogged American resistance had slowed up the German advance, the Allies were able to increasingly exert their advantages in tactical airpower and destroy the German forces on the ground as the weather improved. The Allied counterattack in early January succeeded in pushing the Germans back, and by the end of the month the Allies had regained the positions they held six weeks earlier.

The German offensive had totally failed and would ultimately prove to be the last major attack Germany could mount in the west. Defeat was catastrophic for Germany; The Battle of the Bulge in the Ardennes shortened the war and essentially ended Germany's ability to resist in both the east and west, sacrificing men, material and resources they could not afford to lose. When the Soviets launched their own winter offensive in January, they swept aside German resistance and advanced 300 miles closer to Germany in a matter of weeks.

By the end of January, the bulge in the Allied line, from which the battle had drawn its name, was completely closed and the Allies were ready to once again ready to resume their advance. The Allies could offset the losses they'd incurred, but Germany simply couldn't. Antwerp had not been taken, and the Allies were starting to bring increasing supplies through the port to feed their own war machine. This had made the city a target for the German V1 and V2s, limiting the capacity of the docks and inflicting many civilian casualties. But the port never ceased operating entirely.

The German attack had delayed the Allied plans to build up to attack the Siegfried Line of German defences to the west of the Rhine through forcing the diversion of forces to stem the German attack, but towards the end of January plans were put back into effect to prepare to move the frontline deeper into Germany. Operation 'Blackcock' was launched by British troops from XII Corps in the Roer Triangle, the region formed by the towns of Roermond and Sittard in the Netherlands and Heinsberg in Germany. The attack was a success, but the fighting was still fierce, with more than a thousand British casualties. Two Victoria Crosses were awarded, both posthumously, to Fusilier Dennis Donnini and Lance Corporal Henry Harden for their bravery.

The operation's success created the opening for the next major offensive, where 21st Army Group as a whole and the Americans would again combine in simultaneous attacks to drive the Germans back to, and beyond, the Rhine River.

JANUARY 1945

Sun	Mon	Tue	Wed	Thu	Fri	Sat
..	1	2	3	4	5	6
7	8	9	10	11	12	13 Operation 'Blackcock' begins
14	15	16	17	18	19	20
21	22	23	24	25 The Battle of the Bulge ends	26	27 Operation 'Blackcock' ends
28	29	30	31	..	..	..

MONDAY
08

Ground crew sweep snow from a North American Mitchell Mk II of No. 320 (Dutch) Squadron RAF at Melsbroek (B58), Belgium, in prep for a mission, 8 January.

THURSDAY

11

The 484/139 (Mixed) Heavy Anti-Aircraft Regiment defending Brussels against V1 flying bombs on a cold 11 January. The regiment had initially defended West Yorkshire and the north Midlands until they became the first British mixed gender fighting unit to be deployed overseas.

THURSDAY

11

A soldier of the ATS, serving with 'A' Troop, 484/139 (Mixed) Heavy Anti-Aircraft Regiment, at her position in the control room at Haecht, Belgium, 11 January.

SUNDAY

14

A 6th Airborne Division sniper on patrol in the Ardennes, wearing a snow camouflage suit, 14 January. By this point the momentum in the Battle of the Bulge had shifted, and the British ground forces were more involved in the Allied counterattack.

TUESDAY

16

5.5-inch howitzers of 236 Battery, 59th Medium Regiment, Royal Artillery, firing at dawn, before 12 Corps' attack in the Roer Triangle in the Netherlands and Germany as part of Operation 'Blackcock', 16 January.

TUESDAY

16

A soldier from the 9th Battalion Durham Light Infantry fires on German positions from a ruined house in the village of Bakenhoven, the Netherlands – the first village and German strongpoint to be captured during Operation 'Blackcock', 16 January.

TUESDAY
16

White-washed Cromwell tanks of 7th Armoured Division, having successfully crossed the Julianakanaal, roll through the streets of Dieteren in the Netherlands, 16 January.

THURSDAY

18

Infantry of the 6th Cameronians, part of the 52nd (Lowland) Division and with supporting armour, on the move near Havert, Germany, just across the Dutch border, on 18 January.

SATURDAY

27

Men of C Company, 1st Battalion Royal Norfolk Regiment, queue to be served at a Salvation Army Mobile canteen near Mierlo, the Netherlands, on 27 January. This canteen had been in continuous service since it came ashore on the beaches of Normandy more than six months earlier, and was the furthest forward of any in the advance. The red marks on the image were made by the original War Office censor to hide potentially valuable military information.

MOBILE
CANTEEN

FEBRUARY

February 1945 saw the Allies poised to go back on the offensive against the Germans. After the failure of Operation 'Market Garden' the previous year, Eisenhower had reverted to his initial broad front strategy and aimed to launch an attack across the Rhine River into the Ruhr industrial heartland of Germany. This first required that Allied forces occupy and control the whole of the west bank of the Rhine. Operation 'Veritable' was the codename for 21st Army Group's role in a pincer movement designed to trap the German defenders. They would attack in the northern sector and clear the ground between the parallel rivers of the Maas and the Rhine.

However, it would not be easy; 21st Army Group had to overcome several natural obstacles as well as the Germans. They had to fight through the Reichswald, heavily forested terrain squeezed between the rivers, as well as across ground that was underwater after deliberate flooding, shrinking the opportunity for manoeuvre around German defensive positions. At the same time, even the dry ground was thawing and turning to mud under the weight of armour crossing it. This, combined with towns fortified by the German defenders, reduced Anglo-Canadian advantages in manpower and armour.

Yet the Allies did have a major advantage in air superiority over the battlefield. On 7 February more than 750 RAF heavy bombers hammered the towns of Kleve and Goch with high explosives. More than a 1,000 artillery pieces then started a barrage designed to destroy the German defences throughout the Reichswald, and to erode their morale and willingness to fight. On 8 February, the battle was launched. While advances were made, the expected pace was slower. Infantry and armour worked in close cooperation, and the Crocodile flamethrower tanks were used with particularly devastating effect against German fixed defences. The German decision to flood the land around the rivers backfired when it rendered their own minefields ineffective, and the British and Canadians were able to use the amphibious Buffalo tracked vehicle to advance. The Reichswald was cleared, Kleve and Goch captured. After that, the British and Canadians paused to regroup, before driving towards Xanten in Operation 'Blockbuster', and the US 9th Army advancing from the south as the other half of the pincer.

Meanwhile, across Europe plans were already being made for the post-war world. Yalta, a seaside resort on the Soviet Union's Black Sea Crimean coast, was the scene of the second and last wartime conference between the 'Big Three' Allied war leaders: Churchill, Roosevelt and Stalin. It was held between 4 and 11 February 1945 and was designed to decide on the final strategy of the war against Germany and Japan and settle the post-war future of Europe.

The agreement made at Yalta was controversial. In the aftermath of the conference, both Churchill and Roosevelt, who was ill and would die just two months later, were criticised for their seemingly passive acceptance of Soviet domination of Poland and Eastern Europe, and for agreeing to Stalin's demand that all former Soviet prisoners of war, including thousands who for whatever reason had changed sides and fought in German uniform, be forcibly repatriated. There were fears that if this was not agreed upon, then the Soviets might prove highly obstructive when it came to repatriating Western prisoners of war the Red Army had liberated during their advance on Germany from the east.

Yet at Yalta, Stalin agreed to collaborate in the establishment of the United Nations Organization, a key project for Roosevelt. Stalin also agreed – reluctantly, due to the huge effort of Churchill and the British Foreign Secretary Anthony Eden – to France having an occupation zone in defeated Germany. With the atomic bomb still untried and the prospect of heavy American, British and Australian casualties in an invasion of the Japanese home islands, the promise of Soviet participation in the war in East Asia was seen as a great coup.

FEBRUARY 1945

Sun	Mon	Tue	Wed	Thu	Fri	Sat
..	..	..	..	1	2	3
4 Yalta Conference begins	5	6	7	8 Operation 'Veritable' starts	9	10
11 Yalta Conference ends	12	13	14	15	16	17
18	19	20	21	22	23	24
25	26	27	28	..	..	..

THURSDAY
08

A Sherman flail tank supports infantry of the 2nd Glasgow Highlanders at the start of Operation 'Veritable', 8 February. In the background are American gliders that had landed during Operation 'Market Garden' in September 1944.

THURSDAY

08

The German town of Kleve, photographed from a low-flying Auster aircraft, a few days after the major Bomber Command raid on 7–8 February 1945. The raid had been carried out as a prelude to Operation 'Veritable', the British and Canadian advance to the Rhine.

THURSDAY

08

Infantry and armour in action in the Reichswald area at the start of Operation 'Veritable', 8 February. A variety of tanks were used to support the advance, including flamethrower tanks in case the infantry encountered German concrete pillboxes.

FRIDAY

09

Churchill, Roosevelt and Stalin photographed in the courtyard of Livadia Palace, on 9 February, during the Yalta Conference. The three leaders met at Yalta, in the Soviet Crimea, to decide on the final strategy of the war against Germany and Japan and settle the post-war future of Europe.

SUNDAY

11

Churchill tanks of 6th Guards Tank Brigade and infantry of the 2nd Gordon Highlanders in Kleve, 11 February. The tanks and infantry worked in close cooperation to clear German defensive positions.

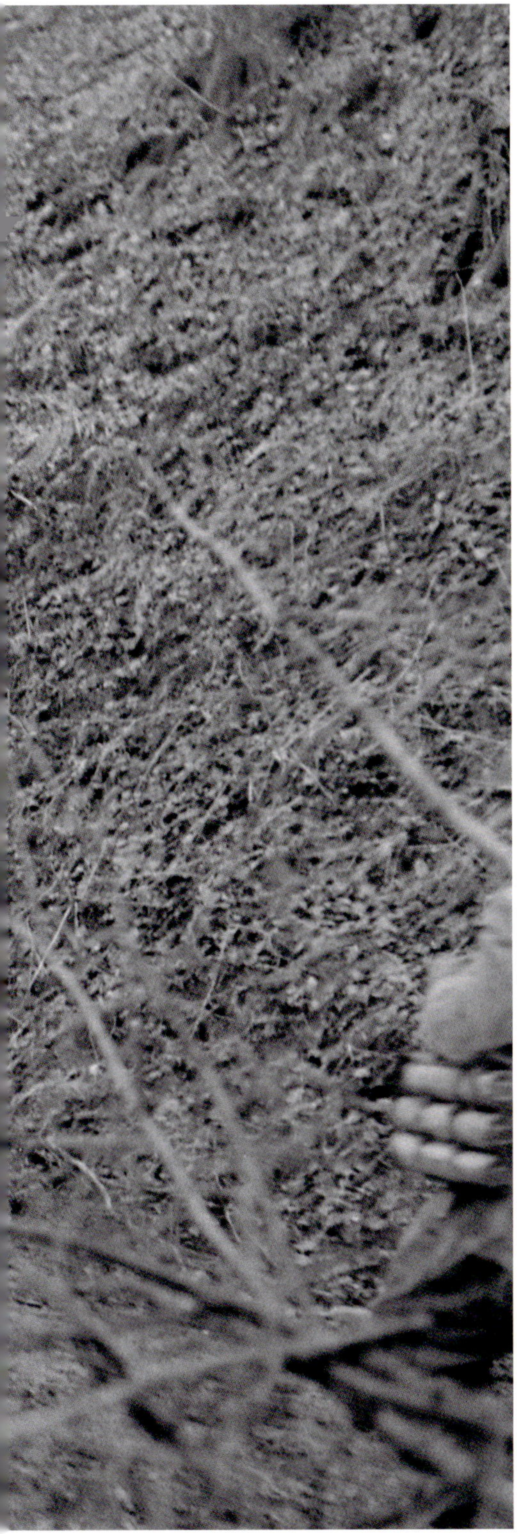

WEDNESDAY

14

Troops of the 2nd Battalion, Gordon Highlanders moving forward to secure and occupy Kleve once the main advance had moved on, 14 February. The Gordons are accompanied by a stray goat that persisted in following them.

SATURDAY

17

Sherman tanks of 10th Canadian Armoured Regiment (Fort Garry Horse) with infantry of the Royal Regiment of Canada massing in preparation for the assault on Goch, 17 February.

WEDNESDAY
21

Sergeant J Welch of 15th (Scottish) Division firing from the ruins of a house in Goch, 21 February.

BEVAULIN
B.V.-
ARAL

WEDNESDAY

28

Sherman tanks of the 4th County of London Yeomanry pass one of their own burning tanks in Uedem, Germany, 28 February.

MARCH 1945

Operation 'Veritable' continued into March 1945, with fierce fighting continuing even once clear of the Reichswald. 'Veritable' concluded with Allied victory in early March, but the pace of the advance had been slower than expected, with the intensity of the German defence and the casualties incurred being greater than anticipated. The Germans withdrew across the Rhine and had blown the bridges behind them by 10 March – leaving 230,000 of their own soldiers on the west bank to be taken prisoner by the Allies. At the same time, the bombardment of Germany – and the German targeting of Britain with V weapons – continued.

The Rhine represented the next great obstacle for the British. Late on 23 March 1945, Montgomery launched Operation 'Plunder', as part of a coordinated set of crossings to get across the river in the area of the town of Wesel and drive deeper into German territory. Montgomery had planned the attack as a three-army assault, including an airborne assault, a 4,000-gun artillery barrage, and with tactical airpower being provided by British and American bombers. Thousands of tonnes of supplies were delivered, including huge amounts of bridging equipment. From 16 March, 36 Royal Navy landing craft were brought forward by road, all hidden by a massive smokescreen.

Under the cover of a 4-hour barrage from 4,000 artillery pieces and air attack throughout 23 and 24 March, Allied troops began to cross by multiple means, including rafts, floats and LVT-2 Buffalo amphibious vehicles. Initial resistance was light but soon intensified.

The amphibious crossing was supported by Operation 'Varsity', the largest airborne operation in history to be conducted on a single day and in one location.

The British 6th Airborne Division and the American 17th Airborne Division – some 16,000 paratroopers – were to be dropped behind enemy lines and seize key objectives. The lessons from 'Market Garden' had been well learned; the troops would drop only a short distance behind German lines so that the ground forces would be able to reach them quicker. They would also all be dropped at once in a single lift, rather than in recurring drops several hours apart. Supplies would also be delivered quicker.

In total, 541 transport aircraft, and a further 1,050 troop carriers towing 1,350 gliders, formed an enormous air armada that stretched more than 200 miles in the sky and took 2 hours and 37 minutes to pass any given point. The troops began dropping at 10am on 24 March, once the ground forces were already ashore on the east bank of the river. Despite early opposition, the airborne troops took their objectives and fought off German counterattacks.

The operations were a success. Churchill himself observed the crossing – and later went over himself to symbolically have lunch on the east bank of the Rhine. By 27 March, the bridgehead across the river was 35 miles wide and 20 miles deep. Nearly six years after the outbreak of the Second World War, the British were across the Rhine and poised to punch deep into Germany. This began a period of rapid, if still difficult, advance for Montgomery's 21st Army Group in the weeks ahead.

MARCH 1945

Sun	Mon	Tue	Wed	Thu	Fri	Sat
..	..	..	..	1	2	3
4	5	6	7	8	9	10
11 Operation 'Veritable' ends	12	13	14	15	16	17
18	19	20	21	22	23 Operation 'Plunder' begins	24 Operation 'Varsity'
25	26	27 Operation 'Plunder' ends — The last V2 rocket strike on the UK	28	29 The last V1 strike on the UK	30	31

THURSDAY

01

A Sherman Firefly tank seen through an archway in the ruined town of Uedem, during the advance to the Rhine, 1 March.

SATURDAY

24

C-47 transport planes release hundreds of paratroops and their supplies over the Rees-Wesel area to the east of the Rhine in Germany as part of Operation 'Varsity'. This was the greatest airborne operation of the war. Some 40,000 paratroops were dropped by 1,500 troop-carrying planes and gliders.

SATURDAY

24

Troops stand on a Sherman Crab flail tank to watch Allied aircraft over Weeze, Germany, during the Rhine crossing, 24 March. The armada carrying the airborne troops stretched 200 miles, and took more than two and a half hours to cross any given point. Like these troops, Churchill watched them pass over at Montgomery's headquarters at Xanten.

SATURDAY

24

Men of the 1st Cheshire Regiment on the east bank of the Rhine at Wesel on 24 March, after crossing the river in Buffalo amphibious vehicles.

SATURDAY

24

British commandos of the 1st Commando Brigade man two Vickers machine guns in the shattered outskirts of Wesel. The 1st Commandos had formed the spearhead of the British assault by making a surprise crossing in assault craft on the night of 23–24 March under a barrage of 1,500 guns.

MONDAY

26

Churchill takes his first steps on the east bank of the Rhine, south of Wesel, on 26 March after the successful Allied crossing. Behind him is Lieutenant General William Simpson of the US Army, Field Marshal Sir Alan Brooke, the Chief of the Imperial General Staff and Field Marshal Bernard Montgomery. Also visible is Rhona Churchill, the *Daily Mail* journalist, who became the first British woman to cross the Rhine in wartime. She also became the first British journalist to visit Soviet-occupied Poland after hostilities in Europe ended.

MONDAY

26

Royal Navy and Army personnel watch guns being towed across the Rhine after completing building of the first Bailey bridge. Montgomery credited the ability to build bridges quickly to move men and material over water obstacles as a major factor in the victory of 21st Army Group.

MONDAY

26

In a deliberate and symbolic act following his crossing, Churchill sat down to a picnic lunch on the east bank of the Rhine with Montgomery and Sir Alan Brooke, 26 March.

TUESDAY

27

The ruins of Hughes Mansions on Vallance Road in East London following the explosion of the last German V2 rocket to fall on London, 27 March. 134 men women and children were killed in the strike. After the successful advance of 21st Army Group, the launch sites were overrun.

FRIDAY

30

Comet tanks of 11th Armoured Division in a devastated German town, 30 March. The Comet was considered an improvement on the Cromwell tanks in use by the British Army and entered service in December 1944. 11th Armoured Division were the first formation to receive them.

APRIL

Once 21st Army Group was across the Rhine in strength, towns in Germany began to fall quickly. Osnabrück was captured on 4 April, with the British having faced little resistance, but other towns and cities proved harder targets. At the Battle of Rethem on 11 and 12 April, as the British advanced north from the Weser, the 53rd Welsh Division lost 230 men clearing the crossing of the River Aller. Despite the casualties, the advance continued, and Celle in Lower Saxony was occupied by 15th Scottish Division on 12 April.

Prisoner of war camps were also liberated during the progress across north-west Germany, releasing British soldiers and airmen who in some cases had been in captivity for five years. But it was the discovery of another camp in April 1945 that had a seismic effect on the British. On their line of march, as they fought their way to the Baltic, lay a camp at a place called Belsen. A German envoy had arrived in British lines to explain that in the camp diseases such as typhus were endemic. The Germans proposed declaring it an open area to prevent fighting and reduce the risk of inmates escaping and spreading disease to soldiers and civilians. The truce was accepted, and on 12 April a 48-square-kilometre exclusion zone was placed around the camp with the area being declared neutral. The Germans, and the Hungarians they were employing, would remain only to guard the camp until the British arrived, after which they would be allowed to march back to their own lines with their weapons.

On 15 April, three days after the truce and with strong German resistance still being met in the area around the neutral zone, the first British troops entered the camp at Belsen. They were utterly unprepared for what they found. There were more than 60,000 emaciated prisoners in desperate need of immediate help. Worse still, 13,000 corpses lay around the camp, unburied and rotting.

Dick Williams, one of the first military personnel into the camp, recalled its nightmare atmosphere:

> You just couldn't understand that all those people could be there and yet everything was so quiet...It was just this oppressive haze over the camp, the smell, the starkness of the barbed wire fences, the dullness of the bare earth, the scattered bodies and these very dull, too, striped grey uniforms – those who had it – it was just so dull... Everything seemed to be dead. The slowness of the movement of the people who could walk. Everything was just ghost-like and it was just unbelievable that there were literally people living still there.

It was unlike anything the British soldiers had ever seen. The soldiers photographing and filming what they discovered called it a 'horror camp.' In his radio report from the camp that day, the veteran BBC journalist Richard Dimbleby, who had been accompanying the troops, said simply, 'This day at Belsen was the most horrible of my life.'

While the British continued the fight elsewhere, at Belsen they rushed to stabilise the situation. Their first priorities were to bury the dead, contain the spread of disease, restore the water supply and arrange the distribution of food that was suitable for starving prisoners in various stages of malnutrition. Additional military and civilian medical personnel were brought in to support the relief effort, including 97 volunteer medical students being rushed to Belsen from the UK. Despite all this, a further 14,000 people died after the camp had been liberated.

Elsewhere, after crossing the Rhine, the Canadians wheeled to the north and began liberating the areas of the Netherlands still occupied by the Germans. Dutch civilians were enduring a famine, and to help alleviate the suffering and prevent humanitarian disaster, RAF Bomber Command aircraft dropped food rather than bombs. Across more than 3,000 individual sorties more than 7,000 tonnes of food was delivered.

The Allies continued advancing deeper into Germany each day. For the British, the advance was rapid, 200 miles across northern Germany in three weeks. In the East, the Soviets began the assault on Berlin, and Hitler committed suicide on 30 April. Victory was within reach. The only question remaining was how much longer the Germans would, or could, continue to fight.

APRIL 1945

Sun	Mon	Tue	Wed	Thu	Fri	Sat
1	2	3	4 Osnabrück captured	5	6	7
8	9 Liberation of Stalags XI-B and 357 POW camps	10	11	12 Celle captured	13	14
15 Liberation of the Bergen-Belsen concentration camp	16	17	18	19	20	21
22	23	24	25	26	27	28
29 Liberation of Stalag X-B POW camp	30 Hitler commits suicide in his bunker in Berlin	..	..	..	..	..

WEDNESDAY
04

Commandos of 1st Special Service Brigade in Osnabrück, 4 April.

FRIDAY
06

SATURDAY
07

Above A Sherman tank of the 1st Coldstream Guards, fitted with 60lb aircraft rockets on the turret sides, crossing a pontoon bridge over the Dortmund-Ems Canal, 6 April. The firepower – both on land and in the air – the Allies could bring against the weakening Germans was increasingly significant.

Opposite Soldiers from 11th Armoured Division examine 'Panzerfaust' anti-tank weapons fitted to a woman's bicycle, 7 April. The Germans were increasingly using bicycle-mounted tank-hunting units in the Petershagen area to try and slow 11th Armoured's advance.

THURSDAY

12

Troops of the 1st (Armoured) Coldstream Guards silhouetted against burning buildings in Berge, Germany, 12 April.

THURSDAY

12

Two blindfolded German officers are led through British lines at Winsen, Germany, on 12 April, after notifying the advancing British forces of the existence of infectious disease in Bergen-Belsen concentration camp. Negotiations for a truce had been concluded, under which it was agreed that, in order to contain the disease, a 48-square kilometre area around the camp was to be evacuated and placed out of bounds to combatant units of both sides other than those engaged in relief work at the camp.

MONDAY

16

British POWs at Stalag 11B at Fallingbostel, Germany, welcome their liberators, 16 April.

TUESDAY

17

Josef Kramer, the Commandant of Belsen, under guard, with manacled ankles, being removed to the POW cage at Celle, on 17 April. In September 1945, Kramer and 44 of his former associates at Belsen and Auschwitz were brought before a British military tribunal in the town of Lüneburg. Kramer and ten others were executed for war crimes in December 1945. The rest were acquitted or sent to prison.

TUESDAY

17

A camp inmate, reduced by starvation to a living skeleton, delouses his clothes, 17–18 April.

WEDNESDAY

18

A prisoner, too weak to move as a result of starvation, sits by the wire fence with an expression of agony on his face shortly after the camp was liberated, 17–18 April.

FRIDAY
20

A Cromwell tank of 7th Armoured Division, the Desert Rats, on the Bremen-Hamburg autobahn, 20 April. Hamburg, as a major city, was the target of 7th Armoured. The expectation was that it would have to be taken in bitter house-to-house fighting.

MONDAY

30

German POWs captured by 2nd Gordon Highlanders, near the city of Geesthacht, on the north bank of the Elbe River in Germany on 30 April. The photograph shows a captured German Army major with some of those under his command; they were all young boys, aged between 13 and 16.

MAY

The small city of Lüneburg in Lower Saxony, Germany, 50 kilometres south-east of Hamburg, had been captured on 18 April 1945. The headquarters of 21st Army Group had been established in the Villa Möllering in the nearby village of Häcklingen, and it was here that a German delegation arrived with an offer of surrender on 3 May. The German's Berlin garrison had surrendered the day before to the Soviets, but fighting continued as many Germans tried to break out and reach British or American lines to surrender. The British 6th Airborne Division had linked up with the advancing Soviets on 3 May at Wismar on the Baltic coast. Hamburg was encircled, and duly surrendered.

At Lüneburg, the Germans had wanted to negotiate a partial surrender only, but their offer was rejected. Montgomery instead demanded a total, unconditional surrender of all forces facing 21st Army Group. When the Germans hesitated, Montgomery was unequivocal, and is reported to have said, 'If you do not agree to the...surrender, then I will go on with the war and I will be delighted to do so.' The Germans left to confer and returned the next day in agreement. On 4 May, Montgomery accepted the unconditional surrender of the German forces in north-west Germany, the Netherlands, Denmark and Schleswig-Holstein.

However, this did not bring the war in Europe to an end. Peace only came with the signing of the German Instrument of Surrender, which took place first at Eisenhower's headquarters in Reims in France on 7 May. The document of surrender was signed on behalf of Germany by General Alfred Jodl and came into effect the following day. Wednesday 8 May had been designated as Victory in Europe Day. Europe was – officially at least – at peace. Stalin, however, wanted his own ceremony, not an inherited victory. The ceremony was repeated in the early hours of 9 May at Karlshorst in the eastern Berlin suburbs where a further document was signed – this time by German Field Marshal Wilhelm Keitel with representatives of the Soviet Union High Command present.

The news of Germany's surrender was not surprising. It had been anticipated for some time and people across Britain were on standby to start celebrating the end of the war. The announcement that the war had ended in Europe was broadcast to the British people over the radio late in the day on 7 May. The BBC interrupted its scheduled programming with a news flash announcing that VE Day would be a national holiday, to take place the following day. Newspapers ran the headlines as soon as they could, and special editions were printed to carry the long-awaited announcement. The news that the war was over in Europe soon spread like wildfire across the world. Wild celebrations followed in London, with people and service personnel flooding the streets. But while many celebrated VE Day, for others it was a source of continued trauma. For those who had lost loved ones in the conflict, it was a time to reflect. Amidst the street parties and rejoicing, many people mourned the death of a friend or relative, or worried about those who were still serving overseas. For many of those bereaved by the war, the noise and jubilation as people celebrated VE Day was too much to bear and not something they could take part in.

VE Day marked the start of the political, economic and physical reconstruction of the continent. In June 1945, 50 countries signed the United Nations Charter and pledged to maintain international peace and security. In July, at the Potsdam Conference, the British and the

Americans, and their new leaders, decided with Stalin and the Soviets that Germany would be occupied by the victorious Allies. It would also be demilitarised and disarmed. German industry capable of being used for military purposes was to be dismantled and the defeated country's educational and judicial systems to be purged of Nazi influence. Nazi racial laws and other legislation were to be repealed, and war criminals tried and punished. German society was to be reshaped on democratic lines but the reconstitution of the country as a sovereign state was postponed indefinitely. In the meantime, Germany was to be run by an Allied Control Commission made up of the four occupying powers.

For Germany, it was *'Stunde Null'*, Zero Hour, marking the end of the Second World War and the beginning of a new era. As Montgomery said in his message to British and Canadian troops on that day, 'Let us embark on what lies ahead full of joy and optimism. We have now won the German war. Let us now win the peace.' This was the start of the occupation of Germany; the British would go on to maintain combat units in Germany for another 74 years until 2019.

However, VE Day did not signal an end to the Second World War. Allied servicemen who had fought their way through Europe prepared for their transfer to South East Asia and the Pacific. The possibility of redeployment was a stark reality for many soldiers, and something with which many were preoccupied. BLA, the acronym for the British Liberation Army – the designation for the force sent into action in north-west Europe – was repurposed by soldiers to mean 'Burma Looms Ahead'.

For those Allied servicemen still fighting in South East Asia, and the thousands more held as prisoners of war in terrible conditions, VE Day meant little. The final months of the war in the Pacific saw heavy casualties on both sides, but ultimately ended in victory for the Allies. After the atomic bombs had been dropped on Hiroshima and Nagasaki on 6 and 9 August, Japan's leaders agreed to surrender on 14 August. VJ Day was celebrated in the UK and Germany on 15 August.

For many the supposed peace was an illusion, and fighting continued across the territories of the former European empires, and between the former Allies and their competing visions for the post-war world. For people in Britain, the end of the fighting didn't mean an end to the impact of the war on their lives. Although many things slowly began to return to normal, it took time to rebuild the country and shortages were still felt: clothes rationing lasted until 1949 and food rationing remained in place until 1954. Peace brought its own problems. The huge economic cost of the war resulted in post-war austerity in a practically bankrupt Britain, and the far-reaching political effects of the conflict ranged from the fall of the British Empire to the onset of the Cold War.

The Second World War, and in particular the events between D-Day and VE Day, continue to have enormous resonance in Britain today.

MAY 1945

Sun	Mon	Tue	Wed	Thu	Fri	Sat
..	..	1	2 Berlin surrenders to the Soviets	3 Hamburg surrenders to 21st Army Group	4 Surrender of German forces on Lüneburg Heath	5
6	7 The preliminary German Instrument of Surrender is signed	8 VE Day	9 The German Instrument of Surrender is signed	10	11	12
13	14	15	16	17	18	19
20	21	22	23	24	25	26
27	28	29	30	31	..	..

WEDNESDAY

02

Infantry of 2nd Wiltshire Regiment, 5th Division, supported by Churchill tanks of 6th Guards Tank Brigade, clear a pocket of resistance south of Lübeck, Germany, 2 May. The advance through Germany was no simple victory parade for 21st Army Group, despite collapsing German resistance.

THURSDAY

03

Men of 6th Airborne Division greet the crew of a Soviet T-34/85 tank during the link-up of British and Soviet forces near Wismar on the Baltic coast, 3 May. The link up completed the encirclement of German forces in north-west Germany and Denmark, cutting them off from the rest of Germany.

THURSDAY

03

British Military Policemen giving instructions to German policemen in Hamburg to facilitate the occupation immediately after the city's surrender on 3 May.

THURSDAY

03

Montgomery receives Admiral von Friedeburg and other members of the German surrender delegation at 21st Army Group Headquarters on Lüneburg Heath for the first time, on 3 May.

FRIDAY

04

Montgomery accepting the unconditional surrender of the German armies on the British front and all naval ships in north-west Europe at Lüneburg Heath after the German delegation had returned to agree to his terms in full, 4 May.

FRIDAY

04

German troops using horse-drawn transport make their way towards the British forces in Hamburg to surrender, 4 May.

SATURDAY

05

A Cromwell and Challenger tank of 8th Hussars, 7th Armoured Division, surrounded by German civilians outside Dammtor railway station in Hamburg, 5 May. The British occupation of Germany had begun.

TUESDAY

08

Members of the Women's Land Army celebrate with soldiers in Trafalgar Square, London, on VE Day, 8 May.

TUESDAY
08

View of the crowd in front of the Ministry of Health building on Whitehall in London, 8 May. Prime Minister Winston Churchill addressed the crowd from the balcony, which, like the roof of the building, was decorated with flags. On the right is the Cenotaph.

TUESDAY

08

Churchill waves to crowds in Whitehall on the day he broadcast to the nation that the war with Germany had been won, 8 May.

TUESDAY

08

In Lüneburg thousands of German civilians gathered in the square in front of the Rathaus to hear the official news of the German unconditional surrender, and the end of the war in Europe, on 8 May. A British loudspeaker van was used to relay the news in German. The photographer, Sergeant Norman Midgley, noted that the news was met with absolute silence.

TUESDAY

08

Two small girls waving their flags in the rubble of Battersea, London, on VE Day, 8 May.

TUESDAY

08

Ground crew on a RAF Bomber Command station in Britain return the V-sign to a neighbouring searchlight crew to celebrate VE Day, 8 May.

THURSDAY
10

Bombardier Wilson of 5th Royal Horse Artillery, 7th Armoured Division, uses a Cromwell observation post tank to show off the Union Flag that he carried throughout the north-west Europe campaign, from the Normandy beaches to Hamburg, 10 May. His journey represented that of 21st Army Group, and the drive to victory in Europe.

IMAGE LIST

All images supplied by IWM unless otherwise stated

June 1944: H 39070, B 5114, B 5261, MH 2074, A 24459, A 23938, B 5228, B 5184, B 5251, HU 91464 © Rodger, CL 118, A 24136, B 6060, B 5968, B 6000, B 6124, B 6184; July 1944: B 6722, B 6725, B 7413, B 7441, CE 154, B 8032, B 7759, CH 13551, B 8277; August 1944: B 8496, B 8886, B 9032, B 9231, B 9205, CL 838, B 9464, B 9538, MH 1426, HU 31069, B 9617, BU 70, HU 66477, BU 141; September 1944: BU 272, BU 508, CL 1086, K 7586, CL 1168, TR 2369, MH 2061, BU 1144, B 10172, BU 1109, BU 1119, HU 2129; October 1944: B 10465, B 10890, C 4669, B 10582, TR 2393, B 10814, BU 1217, B 11058, B 11122, B 11374; November 1944: A 26272, BU 1255, CL 1513, B 11576, HU 128166, B 11917, B 12028, B 12260; December 1944: B 12683, B 13038, B 13114, B 13119, B 13124, B 13136, C 4864, B 13230; January 1945: CL 1775, B 13527, B 13529, B 13676, B 13744, B 13712, B 13706, B 13767, B 14143; February 1945: BU 1693, C 4964, BU 1768 , NAM 236, B 14608, B 14595, B 14681, B 14777, B 14933; March 1945: B 14960, EA 59364A, BU 2072, BU 2336, BU 2329, BU 2250, BU 2392, BU 2636, HU 88803, BU 2760; April 1945: BU 3057, BU 3158, BU 3204, BU 3334, BU 3624, BU 3661, BU 3749, BU 3766, BU 3728, BU 4166, BU 4893; May 1945: BU 4990, BU 5230, BU 5084, BU 5145, BU 5207, CL 2538, BU 5411, HU 49571, TR 2876, H 41849, BU 5669, HU 49414, CH 15165, BU 6134

SOURCES

Montgomery to Eisenhower, Situation Report 30 July 1944. M-68, Correspondence File. Papers of General of the Amy Dwight D Eisenhower, Eisenhower Presidential Library

Dick Williams (15437) © IWM

ABOUT THE AUTHOR

Dr Peter Johnston is a military historian and museum professional. He is currently the Director of Narrative and Content at IWM, having previously been Head of Collections and Research at the Royal Air Force Museum and Head of Collections Research and Academic Access at the National Army Museum in London. Peter studied History and Modern History for his Undergraduate and Masters degrees at the University of Durham, and completed his PhD at the University of Kent, focusing on recruitment and culture in the British Armed Forces.

Peter has acted as an expert and accompanying academic on battlefield tours from Flanders to the Falklands, as well as regularly appearing across media channels providing expert commentary and insight.

ACKNOWLEDGEMENTS

No book is written alone, and I'd like to thank IWM colleagues Lara Bateman for their support, guidance and patience during the writing process, and James Taylor for their helpful and insightful comments as editor to make the book be the best it could be. Finally, and most importantly, I am forever grateful and fortunate to rely unconditionally on Hannah, Tilly and Lyra. Without you I couldn't do any of this.